Praise for The Art of T

"Billy W. Merritt IS text message selling. He lives it every day. He is absolutely on point about the importance of communicating with customers how they want to be communicated with. I would highly encourage anyone in car sales (or any sales for that matter), to read this book and take notes. This is the blueprint for how to up your game for the modern times. Anyone who can't take at least one thing from each section of this book may be a lost cause.

Billy has done a fantastic job at taking his real-world experience and expertise and consolidated it into an easy to read and digest book. We should all thank Billy for putting this all down in one place for us and letting us in on how he has been successful. Thanks, man! I appreciate you!" -Trevor Brooks

"I'm new to the car business. There has been nothing that has changed how I thought and acted on the showroom, like this book. While everyone is complaining about their low months, and n no ups, I don't hear them, because this is the best month I've ever had. I'm too busy treating customers and setting appointments to complain. I'll leave the rest of the secrets in the book. I'll talk to y'all later, I have people to text! When I get home, I am going to read the book again. You can't read a book like this just once. Buy in, and cash out, enough said." -Shane Spires

"I feel like Billy Merritt has done a great job of transferring all of his ideas and putting them to paper. If you are in sales of any kind, and you have not read this book, then you are already behind! Stop what you are doing, get this book and do not stop until you have read the entire book! It will change your life and your checking account, it has mine! When you're done, you will understand "The Big Offer." -Chad Walker Gay

"If you are trying to adapt to the next generation of communication and sales, this is a must read! What Billy and his team bring to the table with this technique is amazing!" -Ron Baus

"I've been in the car business for thirty-three years, and I was taught the "old school" way of selling: to give as little information as possible, and to say anything to get the appointment. The Art of Text Message Selling is a true "how-to" book that uses the strength of the internet, and informed customers. The idea of doing what no one else in the market is doing is exciting. I have personally utilized his system doing "super sales" around the country, with much success. If you want to do something that only Billy Merritt and his team are doing, $20 for the book and two and a half hours of your time to read it is a great investment." -Mike Carson

The Art of Text Message Selling:

23 Secrets to Dominate Social Selling

By Billy W. Merritt

ISBN-9781790554089

iv

"To the Go-Getters"

Table of Contents

Praise for The Art of Text Message Selling

Forward

By Peter A. Salinas

Billy Merritt is a long-time friend, and when he called me, I was glad to hear from him. He had scheduled a hosted automotive sales event, using his popular text message marketing systems. I was very familiar with his program, and he asked if I could back up his team and field some texts and set appointments for a few hours. His marketing efforts had been so successful that the sales team was having difficulty fielding incoming texts and managing the ever-growing floor traffic. I said sure, and he made me an administrator. Within minutes, the incoming texts began rolling in.

That's when things got interesting. My smartphone starting pinging like a seat belt warning chime. I started texting prospects, gathering some information, and another one would come in. Then another, and another. Within thirty minutes, I had communicated with twelve different individuals and set six appointments that would arrive at the dealership in the next thirty-six hours. For the next three hours, it was more of the same. Constant texts back and forth, and sure enough, an appointment got set. The prospects were eager to come in. They were glad to provide multiple points of contact for follow-up and appointment confirmations. I got tired and called it quits at about 10:30 p.m. I had to set my phone to silent, because the incoming texts continued well into the night. That was my full-immersion experience with "The Art of Text Message Selling."

I was very flattered and honored that Billy asked me to write the Foreword to his book. In my thirty-seven years as a journalist and automotive communications specialist, I've never been asked to write one before, and I'm smiling right now, because not only do I get to do what I do best, but I get to do it for a book about sales, in the industry I love.

So much has changed in journalism and the automotive industry in the past four decades, and I'm not going to bore you with a rehash of things you already know. Suffice it to say, I started writing on manual typewriters, and knew dealers whose CRM was an index card file box often filled with Post-It Notes and business cards with phone numbers written on the back.

But with all the changes, and the power of connectivity, some things in sales have not changed. It's still important to attract the attention of people who may want to buy a car. It's important to communicate using the method they most prefer. It's important to respond quickly, coherently, and offer them value.

Billy Merritt's "The Art of Text Message Selling" details exactly how to use today's preferred method of communication as effectively as possible. I can tell you from first-hand experience that his marketing tools, methods of engagement, and paths to the sale, work. They work so well, that it may keep you up at night.

Peter Salinas is an automotive communications specialist based in Sarasota, Fla. He has more than 37 years of experience as a journalist, most of that time covering the domestic automotive and new and used vehicle retail industries. He was managing editor of both Used Car News and Dealer Business Journal

The Art of Text Message Selling

The 23 Secrets You Must Use to Remain Relevant in Today's Digital World

Introduction

Why all the fuss about text? Text messaging has changed the world, and how the world communicates. We are currently going through the biggest revolution in the sales force, since the Internet itself became an integral part of our lives.

When I say "text" in this book, I am referring to the act of composing and sending electronic messages between two or more users of mobile phones, tablets, desktops/laptops, or other devices. I am including chat, and any instant message, or direct message used to communicate with customers.

DISCLAIMER: Importantly, sending existing and prospective customers text messages is regulated by federal, and in some cases, state laws and regulations. There are fines and penalties for doing it improperly. Therefore, it is incumbent upon dealers, their third-party marketing partners, and their employees to engage in the practice lawfully. We strongly encourage working with legal counsel or an accredited consultant in developing written policies and procedures to ensure legal and regulatory compliance and making sure those practices are followed carefully.

Text Message Selling is vital to your survival in sales. Learning the Art of Text Message Selling will make you the most valuable player on the team and secure your financial future for the rest of your life. Your spouse, children, and grandkids will be forever financially secure because you learned the Art of Text Message Selling. Sales as a profession is ever-evolving, but Text Message Selling has

1

become paramount, and it's here to stay. Text messaging has all the advantages of a voice call, but with a much-higher delivery rate. Text is faster and less invasive than a voice call. This makes it the preferred communication medium for today's customer.

People may not answer your call, but they read your text messages. Watch the way people look at their phones when their notification goes off. They can't help it. They must look. It's the perfect tool to capture the attention of the customer. Attention is the first step in any sale ever made. The "art" in The Art of Text Message Selling is taking that attention and building on it by giving the customer what they want, to get what we want.

It is important to understand that regardless of what your product or service is, you are a salesperson, whether your name tag says so, or not. If your income depends on something being sold, for your job to exist, you need to embrace the role of salesperson. You can call yourself a product specialist, service provider, trainer or advisor, but if you need a sale, a contract, or a fee to exist, you're in sales.

Simply put, selling in today's marketplace will demand that you know, and master, *The Art of Text Message Selling*. It doesn't matter what you are selling: cars, furniture, houses, rental property, books, lumber, computers, or anything else. Whatever your service, whatever your product, your customers have phones, and you need to be texting them. This is going to become imperative, as car dealers sell into the future. There are thousands of people in your market who will buy from you, but you must have their attention first. There are many ways to get their attention and have them texting you, including Facebook ads, Google ads, website ads, and organic text conversations. Regardless of how you get them, you must know how to get them to your lot and take them down the road to the sale.

Your road to the sale may be different than mine, and that is fine. I am not teaching a road to the sale, here. What I am going to do is show you how to turn "texters" into appointments that show up. There are rules to text message selling. These rules are powerful. They will make you a force in your market. They will allow you to give the customer what they want, without giving away your profit. Your profit is important, and you deserve to keep it.

This book will detail 23 rules for successful Text Message Sales. If you read, understand, and put these rules into practice, your customers will be happy to stop what they are doing, to visit your place of business. More importantly, they'll be happy to buy from you. You will set yourself apart from the competition and be the leader in your market and industry. I am going to show you how to focus on what the customer wants and get what you want. You will achieve this by disregarding some long-held beliefs about selling and information. For decades, possibly centuries, "experts" have taught salespeople to withhold and hide information from the customer. *"You don't want to give them all the information. They won't come in." or "They will just take your information and go shop somewhere else."*

First off, it's time to reevaluate what we know, and what we believe we know about sales. The "way things used to be" is not how things are "now," and if you try to do it the old way, you are going suffer. It's time to forsake the ways that we operated in the past and embrace the future. We need to be more concerned with helping the customer get enough information to decide, than we are about whether the customer is going to shop with us. The more helpful we are to the customer, the more likely they will buy from us.

The Sacred Cow Must Die

Before we learn the 23 Rules, we must first kill a sacred cow. A sacred cow is an idea that is unreasonably held above reproach. Put simply, it is a lie we allow ourselves to believe. Today, we stop believing this one lie that prevents too many salespeople from going from good to great.

These are commonly held beliefs: *"You should not give your customer all the information they want over the phone, or via text." Some "experts" teach their trainees not to text their customers at all. They say: "A real salesman will get them on the phone, and get them in. The customer is looking to get all the information over the phone, so they can take it to your competition. If you tell them everything they want to know, they won't have any reason to come to you. You are giving them all the ammunition they need to buy from somebody else."*

These sales gurus tell us to give customers "just enough" information to keep them interested. All you have to do is explain to them that to get the best deal, they must visit the dealership.

This is an antiquated view of placing the desires of the company above the desires of the customer. It is a sacred cow that should be slaughtered. Here's why. It is fear-based. The fear is that if we give them too much information, we will somehow lose the sale, or even worse, sell a car and not make any money. It is just not true. You can give the customer everything they want, and more, and still hold gross.

The truth is the customer is going to shop around no matter how much, or how little, information you give them. *The truth* is, if you don't text your customers, you will lose them to someone who will. *The truth* is withholding any information from the customer will hurt your chances of selling them. *The truth* is your customer has already been shopping around. *The truth* is every customer is an internet shopper with a super computer in his or her hand.

Treating those "internet shoppers" in any other way is counterproductive. It is far more forward-looking to place the needs and desires of the customer above those of the company. Being helpful and providing the customer with information through text message sets you apart from 99% of the competition. Being "different" is desired over sounding and acting like every other salesperson in your industry. Going above and beyond, providing more information than customers even know they need — this is what it takes to be a top producer, dominate your peers, and achieve your goals.

Delivering all the information in the most convenient way possible will convey the transparency you need to obtain trust. Trust is essential in all positive relationships, and make no mistake, sales is about fostering relationships. To build trust, we must not withhold any information from the customer. We must provide it to them in the most convenient form possible. We must go above and beyond what they are asking of us and give them as much useful information as we can. That information will give them more questions, and a need for our assistance.

By doing this, you will increase the number of appointments. It will increase your show rate and closing ratio. A commitment to giving the customer all the information, and a whole lot more, will get you on the right track to start the journey of mastering The Art of Text Message Selling. This will allow you build a huge following of loyal, happy, buying customers — and make a lot of money. Let's don't kid ourselves. Money is important. It is why we do this. Text message masters make the most money.

Avoiding the Mistakes

It is as important to know what not to say and do, as it is to know what to say and do when texting customers. Here are the five mistakes you don't want to make while text message selling.

Never say you don't have it. You are not helping anyone by telling them you don't have something. Our job is to serve the customer, and by telling them you don't have it is not serving or helping them in any way. In fact, it is hurting them. Eighty percent of the leads you get from a call or text will go on to buy a different product than they inquired about. That means, you'll be right 80 percent of the time if you assume that they are not going to buy what they asked about. You need to help them figure out what it is they really need; not tell them you don't have it. A very simple and ethical way to handle this problem is to understand that if you have access to it, you have it. You are going to learn how to be so helpful they will need you to facilitate their purchase, even if it means waiting *for you* to get it built from the factory.

Never say "You can't, or you don't know." You are the expert. You'd better know. In the time it takes to say, "I don't know," you can find out the answer. It is very important that the buyer feels that they are dealing with an expert with all the answers. Be ready to find the answers and solutions to their questions, but never, never, never, say, *"I don't know."* Find the answer as fast as possible.

Don't go for the appointment before you have offered more than one option. As we established earlier, most people who call in or text ask about the wrong product. If they call in on the 2018 Tahoe, keep in mind they most likely will not buy the 2018 Tahoe. So, just giving them a price and asking for the appointment will not help them, and it will not get you what you want — an appointment that shows. We are going to learn to give loads of information that will make them want to come in and see you. Don't go for the appointment before you offer options.

Never correct the customer. Regardless of how wrong the customer is, never correct them. It is an argument you can't win. You are not a lawyer. You are a sales professional. You win when the customer buys. That is the only battle that you need to concern yourself with. The customer is always right, and even when they aren't, we aren't going to point it out, because it will not help us in any way.

Don't try to build rapport. A text message buyer wants information and is not interested in getting on common ground with you. When we provide them with the right information, we build trust. Building trust is much more important than rapport, and will help you sell way more cars, as well.

Don't take it personally. People are going to get emotional, be rude, and ignore you. So what? Don't take it personally. There is no value in being offended. We are going to learn how to serve them and sell them, despite their attitude. We want to win, and we only win when the customer buys from us. Let them be grumpy, or even mean. Remain professional and emotionless. And remember, It's just business.

Don't take yourself too seriously. Yes, this is business, but don't be an actuary. Actuaries use analysis to predict the risk that an event will occur. They help insurance companies decide how much to charge for coverage of various things. Boring stuff. Don't be that guy. Keep it light and cheerful, and your experience with people will be positive.

"Everybody texts, so I am going to learn how to be a Text Master."
— *The Wise Salesman*

Chapter 1: The Big Offer

"The purpose of a one-minute elevator pitch is to describe a situation or solution so compelling, that the person you're with wants to hear more even after the elevator ride is over." — Seth Godin

The Big Offer is your Elevator Pitch — a concise, compelling offer that grabs attention.

If you grasp the importance of the Big Offer and use it with every single customer you ever encounter, you can double your monthly sales and triple your monthly income. This is a really big deal. You don't want to underestimate the power of the Big Offer. It can change your life. If you fail to grasp or put into practice the power of the Big Offer, you will be forced to attempt the great art of selling handicapped, and you will lose big. You will lose to the salesman who does grasp and use it.

The world is very busy and loud. All that noise will drown out an average offer. Your offers and claims must be seen and heard, if you have a chance of getting a car buyer's attention. They have to stand out. They must be grandiose and over the top. Anything else is useless. They can't buy from you if they don't know about you, and what you have to offer. That's why "The Big Offer" is so important. You must convey that your offer is a really big deal. If you aren't making big claims, no one is going to notice you.

It is a good thing when a customer asks for a price on your product. It means they are interested and would like some more information. Let's give it to them. Let's take what they want, information, and turn it into an appealing big offer that they will almost always say 'yes' to. Anytime we have the customer saying 'yes,' we are headed in the right direction. Let's offer them more photos of the product; a demonstration video; a free consumer report; available financing options including payments; and an appraisal on their current product. Be it a house, a car, a watch, a phone, or whatever you are selling, you can make a Big Offer. What are some things that you know they will want to know before they buy your product? Go ahead and offer those things before they ask.

"Hey, Mr. Customer, Thanks for responding to my ad about the home listed for sale on Apple Drive. Did you know this house is priced lower than the last three houses that sold on Apple Drive recently? I am sure it will sell fast at this price. If you like, I'd be happy to send you some more pictures of the interior and exterior. I can also send you a walk-through video, so you can appreciate the flow of the layout. I'll gladly get you some finance options and low payment options as well. I can even send you an official appraisal on it. Would you like an appraisal on your current house as well? Would any of this be helpful?"

The sales professional willing to offer all this will win, and they will win big. They will win the customer's attention, and that is the most important thing. Without their attention, we will never have a chance to get an appointment. The purpose of a text message and the Big Offer is to set a phone call and get an appointment. The Big Offer is vital in this process. It is the most important thing. Nobody responds to average offers and average claims.

Now, just how do we give all this information, while still giving the customer an incentive to make and keep an appointment — our primary objective. By providing all this information, do we make it more or less likely the customer will come in? Did we just arm the customer with enough information to shop your competition?

A customer texting you about your product was shopping when they met you, and they are going to shop you whether you give them the information they are asking for, or not. Make no mistake, they are going to get the information they want. The wise move is to be the most helpful and make the biggest claims and offers. The most helpful sales professional wins the most sales today.

For instance, auto shoppers making an inquiry about your inventory have been shopping and visiting other dealerships, online. In fact, industry studies show that consumers spend roughly 14 hours online gathering information about their vehicle purchase before they reach out via text, chat, or phone. They were not only shopping elsewhere before they contacted you, they will continue to shop after they communicate with you. By exceeding their expectations, what you have done is turn their heads toward you. You've shown them you are willing to help in ways they haven't even considered. You've built interest and trust, and it is far easier to sell a car to someone who trusts you.

They are not going to trust you if you don't offer them useful information quickly. They are not likely to trust you, if you tell them they must come in to get a price or payments, or to get trade figures, or get prequalified for financing, before a payment estimate can be provided.

By making a Big Offer, you've set yourself apart from your competition. They feel like they're working with a consultant who has the customer's best interests in mind, rather than a salesperson who's looking out for their own interests. By doing the former, what you've done, is ensure the latter.

I understand that there are some businesses that do not offer pricing for their products online or over the phone. While I believe this is a huge mistake, The Big Offer still works, given this policy. You can make a Big Offer without giving a price. There is a huge difference between offering the lowest price and giving the lowest price. For instance, if a customer asks for a price, we say, "I will be happy to get you the lowest possible price on that car, house, watch, or storage space, and any other choice you may make. We specialize in offering the very best price in the marketplace. In addition to the lowest possible price, I can also get you some pictures, a walk around video, some financing options and some low, low payments. I can even get you an appraisal on your existing product. Would any of this be helpful? I will be happy to get it for you."

That is a Big Offer, and we haven't given up any information that would cause us to lose valuable profit. We simply made an offer. We let the customer know we will get them everything they need to make an informed decision. They don't know it yet, but they are going to come meet us in person, take a test drive, walk through the home, or visit your store, and make a purchase. We know this from experience. However, right now, we are in the trust-building phase. We are offering information and creating value by doing it. This is critical. It is the most important thing we can do to get an appointment that shows up and buys from us.

You must make a Big Offer every time. Right up front — every single time. Your Big Offer is your pitch. Know your pitch well. Get with management and compose a pitch that you will use every single time. Make sure it's big, grand, and extraordinary.

Example of a Big Offer

I founded Unlimited Marketing Solutions in 2007 and called on some of the biggest most successful dealerships across the country. One of my favorite dealers was David Maus. He owned David Maus Toyota, Scion, David Maus Chevrolet, and David Maus Volkswagen. He sold those dealerships to Warren Buffet's company, Berkshire Hathaway, for a reported $20 million.

When I pitched David on my coming to his dealership, I used a very Big Offer: "David, I have the best process in America at getting great credit customers in your showroom, and my specialty is making big gross profit deals on 800 Beacons. I will bring a live DJ to entertain customers, and I'll throw in my call center for free."

Big claims like this got his attention and got me a chance to prove it. I did. Then, when I was in his dealership calling customers, I made them a Big Offer to get them in the door. We offered TVs, cash, car washes, oil changes, and T-shirts. Then I made Big Offers on behalf of the dealership, to the customers. My Big Offers got me in the door, got the customers in the door, made the customers happy, and made the dealership, and myself, a lot of money.

I have done this same thing for dealers across the country. It has worked for me from Washington State to Miami, from Tampa to Hartford Conn., and from Boston to Kingfisher, Okla., and hundreds of locations in between. The point of this story is to make Big Offers. They worked for me and will work for you.

"I hear all these weak commercials and lame claims and I like them, why? Because I know my offers are big and bold. I dominate the offer game." — The Wise Salesman

Chapter 2: Be Fast or You're Dead

"Industrial-age speed won yesterday's war. Digital-age speed will win tomorrow's war. Speed wins."— Gen. Stephen Wilson, Vice Chief of Staff, U.S. Air Force, Arlington, Va.

We have all heard that speed kills, right? The fact is, when it comes the Text Message Selling, if you aren't fast, you *are* dead. God blesses the quick.

A Digital Air Strike study published in January 2018, included data gathered from more than 1,500 mystery shops of automotive dealerships. The findings are staggering, yet present sales professionals with numerous opportunities. Among the highlights (or low-lights, I'd say) of this study were these:

- Only 16 percent of dealerships respond to an Internet lead within 15 minutes.
- More than 18 percent don't respond at all.
- Only 25 percent provide pre-owned vehicle options
- 64 percent don't respond to leads on Facebook or Messenger
- Only 32 percent respond with a price quote
- 53 percent fail to respond with any vehicle information at all

It's clear that if most sales professionals aren't responding to their leads properly, there's little chance they provide the customer with a Big Offer.

Think about this. If you simply respond to Internet leads quickly, provide a Big Offer, and send over whatever options necessary— photos and a walk around video — you are doing far, far more than the overwhelming number of sales professionals in the country! You have set yourself above, and apart from, the rest.

But let's focus on speed and agility. If you follow up a lead within 5 minutes, you increase your chances of converting that lead by 900 percent. When a customer is making multiple inquiries online, the sale goes to the person who responds first, about 50 percent of the time. Speed wins. That same Digital Air Strike study says that 48 percent of car buyers say a faster and detailed response that includes photos and a price quote would make them buy from that dealership, over one that did not provide this information. Simple question, why wouldn't you do this?

Regardless of whether it is important to the customer or not, speed is a perceived value. Replying quickly, handling a problem now, getting the job done fast, has value even if speed was not necessary. If you handle things quickly, the perception of your prospects is you are efficient, agile, respect your job, and respect them.

This means that the best time to communicate with these people is while they are on your site or looking at your advertisement. The sooner the better. A lot of people use autoresponders for this. That's fine. Artificial Intelligence can be very helpful, but AI is not a replacement for a human response. It is, however, a great way to give you a couple minutes to read and assess the lead, then prepare and send your Big Offer. Alerts and notifications need to be sent to you as soon as a lead arrives. That way you will respond in near real-time, improving your chances of gaining customer engagement to near 100 percent.

That's what we want — attention and engagement. We get this by responding with a Big Offer as fast as possible. It's the Big Offer that garners attention and engagement, not asking questions or going straight for an appointment. Remember, the customers do not care what we want. We have to give them what they want, first. We will get what we want later — resulting in mutually beneficial relationship. A solid goal for a response time for every lead is 60 seconds. That may seem extreme, but you aren't reading this book to be average. Now quickly, get extremely serious about being fast.

I run Social Media Customer Acquisition Events for multiple dealerships across the country every week. My Text Team is on call from 6 am -10 pm, 7 days per week. When a lead comes in, they answer it within seconds. If they don't, the customer is on another site looking at another car, and the team member who was responsible for answering the lead is on LinkedIn looking for another job. That's how seriously I take being fast. It is a really big deal.

Be fast my friend.

"I'm woke and clickin' quick ... because I know if I ain't fast ...   I'm dead." — *The Wise Salesman*

Chapter 3: Have a Great Attitude.

"Any fool can criticize, condemn and complain – and most fools do."— Benjamin Franklin

"I am an optimist. It does not seem too much use being anything else." — Winston Churchill

People will pay more for a great attitude than they will a great product, so unless you have all the money you need, you can't afford to have a bad attitude. A product can be shopped. A great attitude cannot. There is nothing more valuable than a positive, smiling, happy person. A positive attitude that persists even when confronted with negativity is priceless. We must be agreeable, even if the customer is not. Your attitude has to be so positive that it even changes the negative conversations to positive ones. How you craft and send texts to others will determine how they text you.

This may seem obvious when selling, but texting makes it too easy to be short, and come across the wrong way. If you are in a bad mood, thinking negatively, complaining, or frustrated with your personal or professional condition, it will come across in your texts, phone calls, and emails. You've heard the expression, "You can hear a smile over the phone." It's true. It is vital that you have a positive attitude and truly value the interests of your customer. It will bubble through in your texts.

Just be positive. It is a force unto itself. You should read Napoleon Hill's *Think and Grow Rich*. Literally millions have read it, and it is one of the greatest selling books of all times. Hill said: *"You are the master of your destiny. You can influence, direct and control your own environment. You can make your life what you want it to be."*

Have a can-do attitude. Be incontrovertibly positive about your customer, regardless of their complaints and stalls. Believe that you can get the appointment. Believing makes it possible. If you say you can't, you won't. If you say you will, you will find a way. Have a great attitude and believe. Be hungry and act hungry. Almost everyone appreciates eager beavers. You must be the hard-working, hungry, hustler putting in the extra effort. Being prepared makes it easier to have a great attitude. If you know, understand, and practice the texting rules in this book, you will be more prepared. Your attitude will be positive. You'll get the appointment, the sale, satisfy your customer, get a referral and do it again.

Go the extra mile to convey your great attitude. Add emojis and smiley faces to your messages. *Would any of this be helpful? I'll be happy to get it for you. It would be my pleasure. :)* You can be clever or witty, but make sure what you send can't be taken in a way that might be interpreted negatively. Don't make a joke not everyone will get. It may leave your prospect confused or put off.

The most successful people in the world have the biggest smile and the best attitude. While it may seem logical that they are happy because of their success, the fact is they are successful because of their attitude. Smile. Take inventory of all the things you have to be happy, grateful, and excited about. Bring that attitude into the text message with you. It will make a big, positive impact on your results.

In September of 2014, I promoted a Huge Event at Robby Roberson Ford in Waycross, Ga. We had tremendous traffic and a showroom full of customers, due to my Big Offer. One husband and wife, we'll call them John and Mary, were very upset when they arrived at the dealership. The general manager asked me to go put out the fire, since I was the one who caused it. Earlier, over the phone, I had offered them *"up to"* $45,000 for their 2014, F150, sight unseen, and they were there to cash in on it.

The problem was, when they got to the dealership, the used car manager had appraised their truck for $35,000, and the salesperson had delivered the offer, blind to the details of my Big Offer. Man, they were mad. John was a career police officer, a very serious guy with a serious white mustache. I am very surprised I even got a chance to plead my case, because they were anxious to leave. In fact, they would have, had the used car manager not had their keys.

With a smile, I introduced myself, "Hey, guys, my name is Billy. I am the guy who sent you the offer on your truck. Thanks for coming in."

"It should be against the law for them to send this kind of crap to me. It's just lies. Robby Roberson Ford should be ashamed," John barked at me.

With less of a smile, but sincere concern, I replied, "I understand sir, but please don't be mad at anyone but me. I am the guy who sent you the offer, and I am the guy who called you on the phone. There is no one here to be mad at, but me. I am the only one responsible for this. It is no else's fault but mine, but please let me explain."

"Well then, it is you with whom we are upset," Mary broke in.

"Yes ma'am, I am the one responsible, but I am a good guy and I can explain."

"No, you can't. This is ridiculous! We need our keys."

"Yes, ma'am. I will be happy to get your keys. May I please explain why I sent you such an offer?"

"Boy, I have got to hear this," Mary snarled.

"Thank you, ma'am." I picked up the post card I had sent them with the Big Offer on it, and said, "John, it says here that you have a 2014, F150 and that you live at 111 Mayberry Oak Circle. Is that true?"

"Yes."

"Well, John, I think it is pretty crazy that I can get that information. I know your name, where you live, and what you drive. It's crazy that I can get all that information on people without their consent. It is actually kind of scary, but you can buy just about any information you want these days." I said with a friendly, great attitude. "But what is funny, John, is I have all that, but I don't know what trim level your truck is, or what condition it is in, or the miles, or what shape the tires are in. So, in order to give you an offer, I use the top-of-the-line trim, lowest possible miles, perfect condition, perfect tires, no dents, dings, scratches or anything like that. And then, I add every option that is in the book. After that, I get the value from KBB using all those hypotheticals."

"Why would you do that?" Mary demanded, to John's approval.

"Ma'am, it is my job to get people to come in this showroom and buy cars. I am what they call a closer. And I am very good at it. In fact, I am the best closer in America. This dealership has paid me to make you happy, and right now it looks like I am failing, but I am not going to fail. I am going to live up to the claim that I am the best closer in America."

I responded before John had a chance to disagree, which I am pretty sure he was about to do, because he chuckled under his breath at that comment, and it didn't sound like a happy chuckle.

I said, "John, what would you have done if I had sent you an offer of $35,000 for your truck, and then called you on the phone with the same offer? What would you have done?"

"I would have thrown it in the trash, and then I would have hung up on you! My truck is worth more than that. In fact, it *is* a platinum! *And* it only has 14,000 miles on it! *And* it has every option you can get on it," he insisted passionately.

I didn't see that one coming. There is usually something real I can use to devalue their trade-in. I did the only helpful thing I can do. I smiled at them both and had an awesome attitude about the situation. After all, they came to buy. It was up to me to do my job. Solve their problem and close the deal.

"John, Mary, I obviously need to take a closer look at your truck, I agree. It sounds like is definitely worth more than $35,000 dollars. I am going to go look at it myself and see just how close we can get to $45,000. I am going to do everything in my power to make this happen. I am committed to coming up with a solution for this. Life is too short to make enemies. I want to make you guys happy."

Mary looked at John and said, "I was committed to giving him hell, but there is something about what he is saying that makes sense, and he keeps looking me in the eyes. It is all about the eyes. I can tell he is being honest. I can see it in his eyes."

It wasn't my eyes. It was my attitude. I kept a great attitude through this very emotional situation. They were very emotional, and I was very committed to having a great attitude. But if she thought it was my eyes, that was fine with me. It was my eyes.

I went and looked at his awesome truck. It really was worth around $40,000, so we offered close to that, and worked everything out. In fact, Mary traded her car, too. You can see an actual video interview with Mary and me on my YouTube channel. Go to youtube.com and search for "Billy Merritt Very Mad Customer." See what she had to say about the whole situation.

"I am positive that being positive is the right thing to do." — *The Wise Salesman*

Chapter 4. Send Photos, Video, and Make Another Big Offer

"You can start right where you stand and apply the habit of going the extra mile by rendering more service and better service, than you are now being paid." — Napoleon Hill

Text message selling requires sending a lot of photos. It is vital that we send good quality and high-resolution photos. Chances are you have a good quality and high-resolution camera built into your phone. If not, stop what you are doing, and go make the investment of a high-quality phone. I use the latest version of the iPhone, and I always upgrade when a new version comes out. I make my living texting, sending photos, sending videos, and talking on the phone, so it is a no-brainer that I need the latest and greatest tools in the market to get the job done. If you are not an Apple fan, no problem. Your phone is your weapon. Use the brand you like, but don't skimp on quality when it comes to your weapon. Choose wisely.

So, we have gotten a lead, responded quickly with a Big Offer with a great attitude, and we have offered to send additional information. Chances are, your customer will indeed ask for more information. That's part of the art. We know if the first three steps are executed properly, the customer will ask for more information.

Let's do it! In fact, let's go the extra mile! Let's do it, whether they ask for it or not. We are going to "Wow" them with information. At the very least, they will know we are not an average salesperson. We are going to get their attention. Remember, we must have their attention and interest to move along in the sales process. Let's send them lots of information, starting with an introduction video. If a picture is worth 1,000 words, then a video is worth 100,000 words.

What makes a good intro video?

- Smile
- Introduce yourself
- Talk Positively
- Keep it short (30-60 seconds)
- Offer service, information and assistance

This allows them to get familiar with your name, face, and voice. Now you are a human, not just a salesman. This is very helpful in building trust, and it sets you apart from the competition. We do it because we understand that we must be willing to do what others aren't, and because we are professionals. It also allows us to make another Big Offer, through video, this time.

For an example of such a video, search YouTube for "Billy W. Merritt Text Greeting Video." You should be posting videos to YouTube, as well. It is also an easy way to maximize Search Engine Optimization for your business. Simply link your company's website to each video and use tags and keywords that coincide with your business.

Next, grab your cell phone and start taking photos of the product they inquired about. Take a lot of photos. Show your product from several angles. From the front, back and both sides. Be sure to send them as high resolution, so that the prospect can zoom in on any part of the photo. Fuzzy photos are turn-offs. Then take photos of similar products — a little bit smaller, a little bit bigger. Send photos of products that are a little more and a little less expensive. It is very important to send options. Over half the time a customer buys a different product than the one about which they initially inquired.

Just a few years ago, you knew Lowe's Home Improvement as a big box hardware store, and Monster as just an energy drink, but now brands have become publishers. They're creating their own content; including their own YouTube channels; that are filled with their own videos. Even furniture companies and drug stores are branding themselves with their own video content on social media platforms, as well as their websites.

The biggest winners, like Apple, are the ones who best use video as the connective tissue between the store, the customer, and the website. Everyone who is awake should be following the lead of these video giants. You must be a content producer. The tools are literally at our fingertips. We must take advantage of this and send lots of videos. Videos command interest and engage. Be sure they are of good quality.

After our intro video, it is time to send a demonstration video. It is amazing how so few people take the time to do this. This makes it an excellent opportunity to separate you and your business from the competition.

- Here are some tips for an effective demo video:
- Make another big offer *(This is a really big deal.)*
- Feature the product
- Use the customer's name when possible
- Keep it short (45-90 seconds)
- Keep it light and friendly, not serious and starched
- Use humor if you feel funny.
- Sell your name
- Encourage them to call or text
- Use a microphone *(Audio is as important as the video. Be aware of your surroundings. Get out of the wind. Leaf blowers, sirens, construction, and nearby traffic are all distractions. Avoid them.)*
- Offer to send even more information

Give a solid walk around and/or product demonstration. Don't skip this step just because they are not in person. Most people would agree that it is beneficial to give a $30,000 demonstration on a $15,000 product when demonstrating it in person. It is just as important with text message customers. Highlight options and the special features. Show off your facility. Introduce your managers and staff; the ones willing to smile. (No crabs allowed.)

You want your prospects to have an intimate understanding of your product and how it works — features and benefits, but also of all the people and operations that surround it. Most dealerships have some cool things you can show off: autographed sports memorabilia; a great view of the mountains, a lake, or desert; or a giant, inflatable, purple gorilla. Show them just how friendly the people are, and how comfortable they will be when they arrive.

Keep in mind that it is very important that your prospect sees the same atmosphere in the video, as they do when they arrive. Too many businesses advertise a fast, friendly, helpful process, but don't deliver that when a customer shows up. Be the same person in the video as you are in person. In fact, act as though you have some familiarity with the prospect, because after they viewed your video, they do. One of the greatest compliments I have received was from a prospect that saw me in a Facebook Messenger video and said, "You guys always look like you are having fun and you really do make this easy."

Make the Second Big Offer

In the video you send to the prospect, be sure to include a Second Big Offer: *"Hey, this is April, from April's Interior Design. I just wanted to put a name with a face, so you would know who you are texting, and who to ask for whenever you come down to the store. You reached out at the perfect time. We are having a storewide sale with savings up to 70% off. Here is the sectional sofa you asked about. It has a premium down cushion, covered in hand stitched leather. As you can see, this one is symmetrical, but right here, is the same sofa with one side larger and covered with hand stitched fabric, another popular option. Remember, I'll be happy to send you any more information you want. Just send a text of what you want, or you can give me a call on this number. Thanks again."*

Now the customer has two big offers, a video intro, pictures and a video of several options and killer product demo via video, as well. They know who they are texting, and we haven't asked them one intrusive question. All we have asked of the customer so far is, "Can I get you some more information?" It is crucial that we give, give, give, and offer, offer, offer, before we get what we want. This sets us far ahead of the competition.

If you stopped reading right now and put these first four rules into action, you would have a huge advantage over the average salesperson. But that isn't the point of this book. The point is to give you an unfair, overwhelming advantage and to get you more appointments. We don't want to be merely above average, we want to dominate. Read on!

"The most fun part of my job is turning on my camera phone and instantly becoming a photographer and video producer." — The Wise Salesman

Chapter 5: Stop Texting, Start Calling

"I arrive at my office by 9 am, and I get on the phone. There is rarely a day with fewer than 50 calls, and often it runs to over a hundred. I frequently make calls from home until midnight, and all weekend long." —Donald J. Trump, Art of the Deal, 1987

I cannot stress this enough. The power of text message selling is in your ability to call the customers and get an appointment. Elections are won on the phone. Wars are started on the phone. The phone is the most valuable tool to ever be invented. Learn to use this tool like a true business professional. Being scared to call your customer is insane. Dial their number and be a sales professional.

The purpose of every text message is to set up a call, and the point of every call is to get an appointment. We must gain the prospect's interest, engage them with information. We must close the distance between them and us. We want them in front from of us. We need them to touch, smell and drive my car. Then we need them in our office, so we can make our proposal in person. It is time to use our phone skills and get them in.

"But I thought this was a book about text message selling? It is, and if you want to master text message selling, you better be ready to make voice calls as well. Make no mistake, you need to call every single customer that you text, or that texts you. That's right — call them all. If you aren't calling at least 50 customers per day, you are not even touching the edges of your potential. If you want to have a much bigger commission check next month, increase your call volume.

No technology, text skill, script or Artificial Intelligence can replace the effectiveness of the human voice. It is much easier to show genuine interest, concern, warmth, and understanding with a call, than through a text. You must call them. Let them hear the genuine concern in your voice. Don't be afraid to make mistakes. You have nothing to lose, and everything to gain.

Give them just enough time to receive and view your photos and video. Two to five minutes is a good rule of thumb. Then start dialing. If they answer, great! You are going to introduce yourself and make the Third Big Offer. I prefer to use a Big Event Offer. If we are going to make a big offer, let's make it a very big deal!

Here's an example: *"Hey, Mr. Smith, This is Billy, with Big City Motors, I am calling to make sure you got the pictures and video I sent over. You did? Great! Mr. Smith, I don't know if you are aware of this, but we have a Huge Sales Event going on right now. We have marked every car down to the lowest price ever, and during this limited time event we are paying "X" percent over book value, or $X more for trade ins." (Make sure management is on the same page with your offer.) "This is a really big deal. Is there a chance you can come in today before this event is over? Or if I need to, I can bring the car to you."*

To be a great text message seller, you must be willing to stop texting and start calling. If you make a mistake, or aren't yet a great telemarketer, no problem! You still have their number, and you can continue to text.

If they don't answer, no problem! We have a plan for that, too. We have a plan for everything. We are ready, and we are going to sell them a car, whatever it takes, including calling them all.

"I hear a lot of salespeople making a lot of excuses about why they haven't sold enough cars. I just keep making phone calls." —The Wise Salesman

Chapter 6: Leave a Voicemail

"A pessimist sees the difficulty in every opportunity; an optimist sees the opportunity in every difficulty." — Winston Churchill

Over half of the time, no one will answer a voice call. This is not a problem. It's an opportunity. All you have to do is leave a voicemail and be sure to include a Big Offer.

As you can tell, I could have named this book *"The Big Offer,"* and I almost did. People don't respond to average offers or average claims. Get with management and create a big offer — one on which you can both agree. Here is my favorite. It must be grand and extraordinary. It must be exclusive to you. Average living is a losing strategy, and average offers are even worse.

"Hey, Mr. Smith. This is Billy from Big City Motors. I just wanted to call and make sure that you got all the information I sent over, and to let you know, we are having a huge sales event! We have marked every car down to the lowest price of the year.

"During this limited-time event we will pay up to $4,000 more for trade ins. This is a really big deal, and I don't want you to miss it. If you need any information at all, or if I need to bring this car to you, just give me a call back at this number or text me. Thanks again."

While it may be a President's Day Sale, Black Friday Event, or an Anniversary Sale, the theme is always the same. "We have a Really Big Offer going on right now, but it's for a limited time." It's an event. It's special. It's happening now. If you delay, you might miss it. The best Big Offer always has some pain attached to it — the pain you will feel if you miss it.

The issue, the real crux of the Big Offer, is it must have validity. It must entice with a promise of exceptional value, and it must deliver. Your professionalism, products, services, facilities, and warranties should be world-class. Your voicemail should incorporate all of this. Speak with bold confidence. When they listen to your voicemail, they need to feel your conviction in your message. To have conviction, you must believe in your product, your service, your team and your company. You have to be sold. Sell yourself on your product, service, team and company now. Get sold. If you can't sell yourself, you can't sell anyone else. Get sold. When two people meet, the one with the most conviction will influence the other the most. Be that guy. A.B.C.Y. Always Be Closing Yourself... so you can close others.

"I don't care if they don't answer because I love leaving exciting Voicemails." -The Wise Salesman

Chapter 7: Keep Sending Information, and Lots of It.

"No one has ever become poor by giving." — Anne Frank

Once we have a cell phone number or an active participant in a chat or message service, we need to take full advantage of it. Let's give, give, give. Send loads of information. Send multiple pictures. Send multiple videos. Send multiple photos of multiple cars. If it is a truck, send a 2WD and a 4WD. Send a Regular Cab, Extended Cab, and a Crew Cab. Send photos of gas and diesel-powered trucks.

If they asked about a car, send photos of coupes and sedans and send photos of the 4-cylinder and 6-cylinder models. Send multiple colors. Send more expensive options, and less expensive options. Just keep sending information. It is way more important to send information, than it is to prequalify or gather information.

The point of a text message is to get an appointment. Send them so many options that they have to come in, to sort it all out. Show them that you don't mind giving them lots of information. Show them by providing them with massive amounts of information, that you want their business. Wow them with your willingness to give.

The more information you give them, the more reasons they have, to meet with you. The person who sends the most information wins.

Send them more information than they ever thought possible. Let them know their inquiry about the Altima, Tahoe, or Impala was vitally important to you, and you responded accordingly. By providing them useful information along with the Big Offer, you've given them a reason to meet with you, and meet with you *now*. Wow them with information, and so many videos and photos, that they just had to come in and meet you.

I have had people call me, to tell me to stop sending so much information, which gave me an opportunity to pitch them on coming in. Once I had them on the phone, I was able to close them on an appointment. The purpose of a text message is to set an appointment. The purpose of sending lots of information is to get an appointment. It is always about the appointment.

You have absolutely nothing to lose. People are busy. You have to break through the noise. They are getting offers from every retailer in the world. We have to break through and stand out. Don't be the guy waiting on them to call. Don't be the girl asking them questions. Don't be the fella forgetting about the lead. Be the person who is sending interesting, helpful information. Stand out as the giver.

"Giving is so much better than getting. I get to be helpful, then I get the sale." — *The Wise Salesman*

Chapter 8: Sell the Appointment and Lock It Down

"I am invariably late for appointments — sometimes as much as two hours. I've tried to change my ways, but the things that make me late are too strong, and too pleasing." — Marilyn Monroe, Actress

Let's make our Big Offer so grand that even Marilyn Monroe will show. But let's face it, there are many reasons why someone isn't going to go out of their way to allow you to make a $1,000 commission on them. Traffic. Time. Ball games. Doctor appointments. Fear of salespeople. Carvana. American Idol. American Ninja Warrior. Rent due. Utilities due. I could go on and on. I know you want to high five your buddies about the five pounder, but the point is, your customer has a whole list of things they care about, and your big commission isn't among them.

Therefore, it is vital that you approach their complaints, stalls, and objections with a Big Offer that stops them in their tracks, commands attention, and forces them to come in and learn more about it. Big Offer. Big Offer. Big Offer.

At this point you have made four Big Offers so grand, that if they are even slightly interested in a car, they will give you an appointment. Call and get it.

"Mr. Smith, this is Billy. Did you get all the information I sent over?

"Yes. I have all kinds of information and pictures from you."

"Great! When is the best time for you to come in and take a closer look, and let me take a closer look at your car? I can't wait to see it. I am going to show you how to get the very most money for your

trade-in. I have my favorite appraiser ready to look at it with me. He always pays more than the other appraisers. Is tonight before we close good, or is tomorrow morning best for you?"

If they don't answer leave another Big Offer, then go for the appointment via text.

"Mr. Smith, I would really like to meet you in person and show you some of these options that I have sent over. I may even have some other options here on the lot that you may want to see. When is the best time for you to come down to the dealership to take a test drive and allow me to check out your trade-in? I have my favorite appraiser standing by. He always pays more than the other guys. Is today good, or will tomorrow morning be better? This is a really big event and it ends soon."

As you see, I have several big offers blended in here: favorite appraiser, big event, ends soon, etc. Make your offer special-limited time, 2 days only, limited to the first 10 customers today, biggest sale of the year, low payments, no money down etc. All these things add value to your appointment. We are selling them on why it is worth them stopping what they are doing to come in. Big Offers are so important. I am sold on this being a Big Deal. Are you? You better be. If you aren't, your customers will not be either. People don't respond to mediocre offers, claims and deals. Make it a big deal.

After they have given you an appointment, lock it down.

"Mr. Smith, is there any reason why you can't be here tomorrow at 9:15 am?"

"I can't sit around chit-chatting. I have all these appointments, and a lot of my co-workers sit around having coffee, talking about the sales they didn't get." — The Wise Salesman

Chapter 9: Get Social

"Facebook is the most successful thing in the history of humankind."
— Scott Galloway

Over 200 million Americans have a Facebook account. That is over 70 percent of the population of the country. Worldwide, there are more than 2 billion Facebook users. Facebook and Facebook Messenger are the two most downloaded mobile apps in the world. Instagram, (which is owned by Facebook), Snapchat, and Twitter are all in the top ten. If you aren't getting attention and engaging with people on social media, you are making a huge mistake, and your days in business are numbered.

If someone texts you, find them on Facebook. Send them a friend request. Follow them on Instagram, SnapChat, Twitter, or LinkedIn. The more places they see you, the better.

Follow these Rules of Getting Social.

- Use your profile picture to show what it is you do. I should be able to look at your   profile picture and tell what it is you do. You can take a picture in from of your dealership or in front of a car with magnetic signs on the side. Create your own slogan and add text to your profile picture. "I Sell Cars for Less." Be creative but make it clear to people who see your photo, what it is you do.
- Use your cover photo the same way.
- Post pictures of all your sold customers and the car they bought.
- Post pictures of the inventory as it arrives to your lot. Make it a big deal.

Edit your bio, intro, and about tabs to show what it is you do.

Make a lot of posts that show that you are very knowledgeable in your field. Be an expert and people will see you as an expert. They will call on you when they have a question about cars, or the car business. This is a great way to get a text message conversation going. Once they have asked you a question, answer it, and start with Text Message Rule No. 1 — Make a Big Offer.

- Find me on Facebook and send me a friend request. Billy W. Merritt
- Find me on Twitter and follow me. @billywmerritt
- Find me Instagram and follow me. @billywmerritt
- Add me on Snapchat - billymerrit
- Connect with me on LinkedIn - Billy W. Merritt
- Follow me on YouTube - Billy W Merritt

You want all the attention you can get on social media. The more professional you can be, and portray yourself, the better. The more you can establish yourself as an expert, the better. Being professional is vital, but even more important is being noticed and being known for what you do. If they don't know who you are, it is impossible for them to buy from you.

Get known. Get personal. Many people make the mistake of keeping their personal Facebook page separate from their professional page.

They have lots of kitty, doggie, and children pics, but no customers or cars. That is a tremendous wasted opportunity. Your customers are on Facebook. Stop posting pets and kids and show them that you are the car guy or girl. Establish yourself as an expert in the automotive field. Don't be a salesman, be an expert. Give free advice. Show happy customers. Dominate your space. Get personal.

In some cases, less is more. This is not one of those areas. When it comes to social media, choose quantity and quality. If you must choose only one, choose quantity. How much is too much? There is no such thing. Top-of-mind awareness is the goal. Total domination of the social media space. Omnipresence. Your presence needs to be so strong, that when someone else is making a social media pitch, it you the customer is thinking about. When someone else is making an offer, the customer is thinking about you and your offer. Stake your claim on the social media landscape. Send me a friend request. Give me a like and a follow. I like and follow back.

Hundreds of people have come in to see me, and the first thing they say is, *"I see you on Facebook all the time. I just wanted to come in and meet you."* Then, they bought a car. There is a video of one of these customers on my YouTube channel, just search for Customers want to meet Billy W. Merritt.

"Uh oh! I haven't posted on Facebook in the last 10 minutes. Let me fix that now." The Wise Salesman

Chapter 10: Use Positive Language

"I am an optimist. It does not seem too much use being anything else." ---Winston Churchill

Is there anything worse than a negative attitude and a big mouth? Not to me! I run from it, and you should, too. Remember, people will pay more for a great attitude than they will for a good product. The only way you can convey a great attitude through text message is with positive language. Text is very easy to misunderstand, so keep it simple. Use these terms: It's my pleasure! I've got this! Easiest part of my job! I am the problem solver! Allow me! I'm your boy! I am your girl! Today is your lucky day! Would you consider? I agree! I understand! I'd be happy to! You got it! You bet! It would be my pleasure. I love it when you come to just look. Great idea! I sure can. Done! Perfect! Yes, sir! Yes, ma'am! Of course!

If you want an appointment to show up, you cannot be indifferent. Be bold, excited and positive.

Norman Vincent Peale wrote a book called "The Power of Positive Thinking." I encourage you to read this book. It has sold millions of copies in dozens of different languages. Suffice it to say, Mr. Peale contends we all have the power to succeed, and that comes from our ability to think positively.

Among his many keys to Positive Thinking, he says this: "Whenever a negative thought concerning your personal powers comes to mind, deliberately voice a positive thought to cancel it out."

So, when you're getting ready for a phone call with a prospect, or sending over a text, try thinking this way and use positive language to convey your messages.

Most objections are not really objections. They are simply complaints. The price is too high. I can't come in today. I don't have time. I am just looking. I have to talk to my spouse. I need to think about it. Yada, yada, yada. The easiest and most-effective way to overcome these complaints is to simply acknowledge them, think positively, use positive language, and make them a Big Offer.

"Yes, sir. That is too much for a used truck, I completely agree. The market keeps driving them higher and higher. Let's get you in here and take advantage of this extra money for trade-ins this weekend, before they get even higher."

"Today is your lucky day. I am the problem solver. You got the right guy. Consider this mission accomplished. Allow me to show you how easy this is. That would be my pleasure." — The Wise Salesman

Chapter 11: Carefully Copy and Paste

"If you want to be successful, find someone who has achieved the results you want and copy what they do, and you'll achieve the same results." — Tony Robbins, Author, Self-Help expert

The same scenarios come up over and over, in sales. If you know what's coming, you can have your answers ready. Just simply have the answers saved, so you can copy and paste them right to your text message. But be careful. Take your time and read the questions fully. Make sure you are acknowledging the right questions. When leads are coming in hot and heavy, it can be very tempting to blast the same message back to them all, after all, Rule No. 2 says we've got to be fast, right? Yes, but take enough time to make sure you aren't glossing over the customer's questions or concerns. Always acknowledge what they are asking, and carefully copy and paste with another Big Offer. Don't get ahead of yourself. It is a huge turn-off to have your questions ignored and talked or texted over. Here are some of the most common questions to expect, followed by the answers that I have stored on my phone and on my computer. I simply copy and paste the answer and send the text. These answers are smart, and each contains its own Big Offer. Each generates even more interest.

How much is it?

Response: That one is priced No. 1 in the market at $21,000. In addition to the lowest price, I can also get you some pictures, a walk-around video, some finance options, some LOW, LOW payments. I can even get you an appraisal on your car. Would any of this be helpful? I'll be happy to get it for you. 😊

How much can you give me for my trade in?

Response: I will be happy to get you an official appraisal for your trade in. We pride ourselves in giving the most for trades. During this limited-time event we are even paying an extra $4,000 over KBB for trade-ins. This is a really big deal! When would be the best time for you to bring it in? I want to make sure I have my favorite appraiser here to look at it. He always pays more than the other guys. ☺

What do you have for $x,xxx?

Response: All our cars are nearly new. We have Nissan Altimas as low as $12,888. We could do zero down payment on one of those; and get you some really low payments. Would you consider our Zero Down, Nearly New, Low Payment Program?

Do you have a third row SUV?

Response: Absolutely, I specialize in selling third row SUVs. And I sell them all at the absolute lowest price on the market. In addition to the lowest price, I can also get you some pictures, a walk-around video, some finance options and some low, low payments. I can even get you an appraisal on your vehicle. Would any of this be helpful? (Note: replace "third row SUV" with any specific vehicle they ask for).

But I don't want to be upside down.

Response: I understand. I am going to make sure you aren't upside down. Allow me to handle this for you. When is the best time for you to come in, so I can get my favorite appraiser to look at your car? He always pays the more than the other guys. Plus, during this limited-time event, we are paying off trade-ins, no matter what is owed. This is a really big deal. What time works best for you?

How much down?

Response: How does zero down sound? 😊 We specialize in zero-down loans. What are you most interested in: a car, truck, or SUV.? We are having a HUGE SALE this week. Every vehicle is marked down to the lowest price of the year. Plus, we are paying an extra $4,000 for trade-ins during this limited-time event. Would a zero-down loan be good for you?

How good has my credit got to be?

Response: Credit issues are not a problem. We use every lender in the state, including secondary banks that have options for those with less than good credit. We aren't worried about your credit. What are you most interested in? A car, truck, or SUV? We are having a HUGE SALE this week. Every vehicle is marked down to the lowest price of the year. Plus, we are paying an extra $4,000 for trade ins during this limited time event. Can I get you some more information on this awesome event?

Here is a section of my actual clipboard that I use every day to answer event leads. This is behind the scenes, secret squirrel stuff.

May I have your cell #? If something comes up on my end, I will text you, and if something comes up on your end, you can text me.

Make sure you ask for **Markdown Mark. He** is the director of the sale. He can save you the most money, and he is the one who pays the most for trade-ins. Make sure you ask for Markdown Mark 😊

We want your car, and we will pay big money for it. But only for the next 4 days. Can you make it in by Saturday, so we can make you a big offer on it? Make sure you ask for Buyback Bobby. He is the director of the sale. He can save you the most money and he is the one who pays the most for trade-ins. Make sure you ask for Bobby.

This is a really big deal that you don't want to miss. Is there any way you can come in today? I have a few vouchers left for $5,000 over KBB for your trade, or if you don't have a trade, $5000 off. Just ask for Markdown Mark.

Make sure you ask for Wholesale Hank. He is the director of this Epic Event, and I want him to take care of you, personally. He is the best. He pays the most for trade-ins and he gets the lowest payments.

Make sure you ask for Wholesale Tony. He is the director of this Epic Event, and I want him to take care of you, personally. He is the best. He pays the most for trade-ins and he gets the lowest payments. See Tony.

We want your car, and we will pay big money for it. But only for 2 more days. Can you make it in by Saturday, so we can make you a Big Offer on it? We will appraise your car using www.kbb.com, then we will inspect it, test drive it, check the fluids, tires, dents, dings, Carfax and reconditioning costs, then determine just how big of an offer we can make. It will be very big-our average is $4,000 over KBB.

I want your (insert car). Let's get you locked in. Can you come Monday morning? If not, what day and time is best for you? The sooner the better.

(Dealer address)

(Dealership website)

This is a really big deal. Only 2 days left. Today and tomorrow. You definitely don't want to miss this event. What time can you come?

Make sure you ask for Joey from Georgia. He is the Event Director. He has the vouchers, and he pays the most for trade-ins and gets the payments lower than anyone.

Make sure you see Mark. We call him Markdown Mark. He is the best there is at getting the most for trade-ins; and getting the lowest price for his customers. Ask for Markdown Mark.

Make sure you ask for Wholesale Hank. He is the best I have ever seen at getting the payments where they need to be.

Make sure you ask for Buyback Becky. She is the best I have ever seen at getting the most for trade-ins and getting the lowest payment for her customers. She is awesome!

This is a really big deal! We really are paying up to $5,000 over Kelley Blue Book for trade-ins. But it is limited to the first 50 customers. We need to get you in here Wednesday, if possible. That is the first day of the sale. The first day always has the best deals. Can you come early Wednesday? You do not want to miss this Epic Event.

$5,000 VIP Voucher Reserved. (I add this to the notes when I send them an appointment to confirm through Facebook Messenger)

What is your cell phone #? I will send you some photos of what we have, and a confirmation # for the voucher. Make sure you show it to Magic Mark at the dealership. I told him you are coming. He is a really cool guy, and the best I know at getting you the most money for your trade.

Most of the responses are variants on the Big Offer. Keep sending the Big Offer. Every time you contact them, give them more information. Ask them how you can help? Invite them in to the dealership. You'll develop your own responses, as you see which work better than others. But keep a library, then just Copy and Paste!

"I hear a lot of salespeople complaining they don't know what to say to a customer. I am just over here copying and pasting what I said the last time I sold one." — The Wise Salesman

Chapter 12: Love the One You're With

"The present moment is the field on which the game of life happens. It cannot happen anywhere else." — Eckhart Tolle

Treat every customer like he or she is the only one you have, until you have sent them the best text message you can. Don't jump forward to the next customer too fast. Stay in the present moment with the customer you are talking to right now. Finish your offer. Don't fall into the trap of seeing how many messages you can send, or how many individuals you can reach. The best thing you can do for your future clients is give your current client your full attention. If you don't, you are going to do a poor job and be forced to deal with them in the future, to help them with something you could have explained and overcome NOW.

It is important to be fast, but don't take shortcuts. Make sure your offers (and sentences) are complete. Give each customer your full attention. Eventually, you will have so many customers that you can pick and choose who you want to do business with and fire the ones you do not.

It is very possible to do this. But it takes time, and a whole lot of effort. You must train daily and build a huge audience. You must give every customer the VIP Treatment. Treat everyone like a VIP. They are. Plus, when you treat people like they have lots of money they will spend money with you.

Don't hesitate to impose. Pry, and ask questions. It shows your interest and desire to help. Don't stop until you get answers. If you are afraid of these things, or think it is improper, it is probably because a parent, or some authority figure taught you this. Unfortunately, they were wrong. You MUST be willing to impose, pry and ask questions to get what you want. You will give them so much information, that you deserve the answers you need. Far too many people avoid asking hard questions. Ask any question you need an answer to, and don't stop until you get the answer.

"Someone told me that a lot of salespeople run around and see how many people they can talk to, and how many text messages they can send, in ten minutes. I never even noticed this. I was paying attention to my customer." — The Wise Salesman

Chapter 13: Overcome Objections

"Learn to close, and you will never be without work, and will never be without money."— Grant Cardone

Best case scenario, we are going to get an appointment and get to demo our product, build value, and get the customer in our office in a seated, comfortable closing environment. But we don't always get the best-case scenario. The Big Offer will solve most problems, but not all. This means that you are going to have to live up to your title and be a sales professional. You are going to have to use your closing skills and be a problem solver.

Most objections are not real objections. They are merely complaints. Listening to the customers and acknowledging their complaints is important. Do not ignore them. Do not argue. Do not prove the customer wrong. Be agreeable, acknowledge and be a problem solver. There are thousands of books written about overcoming objections. Grab one and practice what it preaches. Learn to close.

The best advice I can give you is: close the distance. The farther they are away from you, or you from them, the harder it is going to be to close them. Give them a reason to come to you, or you go to them. You must eliminate the distance between you and your customer.

When closing any customer, or anybody, on any pitch or idea you have, always remember to let the other party be right. Let them win. Agree with them. If you are agreeable you can add to the conversation and influence them. If you argue, even if they are 100% wrong, and you are 100% right, you will have zero chance of changing their mind. They will dig their heels in and double down on their position. Be agreeable and offer possibilities or alternative ideas. The three most powerful words in negotiations are "Would You Consider?"

Nobody wins, and everyone loses if you don't get the job done. You are not an information gopher just because you offer information. You are a stone-cold closer, or you wouldn't be reading this book. Be agreeable. Close the distance. Acknowledge their complaints and get an agreement.

"I know I can close this deal." — *The Wise Salesman*

Chapter 14: Use Mass Text

"It is much easier to put existing resources to better use, than to develop resources where they do not exist." — George Soros

As I mentioned in the introduction, there are a lot of methods to reaching text message customers, including Facebook ads, Google ads, Website ads and organic text conversations. Regardless of how you get them, you need a way to send mass texts. You can use a BDC. You can use Facebook Messenger. You can use your own CRM, or you can outsource it.

There are several vendors and third-party leads providers to help you automate this. However you do it, you want the ability to send everyone a message at the same time. This is leverage at its best. As you grow your audience, day after day, month after month, this will be even more powerful. You can send special offers, discount codes, surveys, and most importantly, Big Offers.

This is omnipresence and top-of-mind awareness at its finest. It would take you years to visit 1,000 people. It would take weeks to contact the same people with a voice call. But you can send a text to 20,000 or more, at the click of a button. That's real power. This is leverage. Get your audience together and use mass text.

"Give me a lever long enough, and a fulcrum on which to place it, and I shall move the world." — Archimedes

Leverage is the secret to making what you have, go much further. Just like a crowbar or a lever, mass text allows you to harness the power of a strategic text and move mountains. You can move many people to act with the click of a button. Because we are often dealing with limited ad budgets, mass text is the tool you can use over and over for little to no cost, and radically enlarge your footprint in the market. Innovation has no greater ally than leverage.

Use it often; at least once per month. Don't fall into the trap of believing in overexposure. There is no such thing. If they aren't thinking about your offer, they will be thinking about someone else's. If they don't know about your offer, they can't buy it. We must have their attention. Use mass text to get their attention and get them thinking about your Big Offer.

"I just crafted a very smart Big Offer and sent to 200 people. It is time to start closing the distance on all the respondents." — The Wise Salesman

Chapter 15: Send Them a Secure Online Credit App

"Qualifying for a bank loan isn't rocket science." — Rebecca Lake, investopedia.com

As mentioned earlier, in our best-case scenario, we would like to have our customer in our office to close the deal. This would also be the best place to offer financing, however, there will be times it is necessary to work the financing out before the customer comes in. The dealers who streamline their process, in order to cut down on the time a customer needs to be in the dealership are winning in the marketplace.

Customers used to visit eight dealerships before deciding. Now, that number is less than two. Consumers are getting the information they need, online. If we are to remain relevant in this rapidly changing digital landscape, we must make it easier for the customer to obtain financing. We must remember that it's all about the customer, and what they want. Technology also allows shoppers to securely complete a credit application, completely online. Credit application processes are becoming faster and easier, as new financial technologies emerge. Let's embrace the latest and greatest technologies and make it easier to do business with us by sending our applicant a link to a secure online credit application. Lenders can give you a decision in seconds. The more hoops we can take out for the customer, the more successful we will be. Nobody enjoys hanging out with a salesperson while their credit application is being processed. Speed things up. Move things along. Make things convenient. Send them an online credit app.

Some of the most successful text message sellers in the country write their ads based on Big Claims about financing. Guaranteed approval. No Credit, No Problem! You're Approved. There are many Big Claims when it comes to financing, and they get a lot of leads — the good, the bad and the ugly.

Some like this volume and thrive with bad credit. If you are a bad credit doctor, building ads and getting leads will be easy. Too easy. You're going to be pulling a lot of credit histories. Happy hunting! Send them a secure credit application and get them rascals approved. Make sure that your online application follows all the state and federal laws. Get permission to pull their credit and send it to banks for approval.

If you are at a dealership that steers away from the bad credit, I completely understand. But, very often you will be met with a credit-challenged customer. As soon as you hear the signals of bad credit: *"I got bad credit." "I am financed with Santander." "I have a buy here, pay here, car."* Send them an online credit app and take appropriate action. You may need to focus on a different customer. Yes, I know everyone is a buyer, but if they need some help, I want them to bring the credit app and appropriate stips with them. We are going to be selling cars on Saturday. Lots of them. We don't need to be chasing stips.

When you are creating your pitch, it is important that it include some type of offer about financing and payments. As you know, most car deals are closed on monthly payments. So, it is important that we let the customer know we are financing specialists. We always want to convey that we are specialists, professionals, experts. *"Financing?*

No problem! Easiest part of my job, click here and I will get you pre-approved."

Let's look at our Big Offer again.

You: *In addition to the lowest price, I can also get you some pictures, a walk-around video, and some finance options, with low, low payments. I can even get you an appraisal on your car. Would any of this be helpful?*

Customer: *"Yes, that would be helpful. What will my payments be?"*

If you are going to quote them a number, you better go low. Telling a customer that you don't know, or you can't, is a deal killer. This makes you look like a dummy, not a specialist. If we want this customer to make an appointment and come in, we have to give them something. We have to make it appealing. We have to make another Big Claim. If you are avoiding this question, or saying things like, *"Well, that depends on your credit." "We don't give payments over the phone,"* you are losing.

Give them the benefit of the doubt and send them an online app.

"My pipeline is so full. I currently have 20 people requesting more information from me. I am going to send Mr. Second Chance a link to my online app, so I can cut out some of the extra work, if he can't buy." — The Wise Salesman

Chapter 16: Go for the Video Close

"Whether it happens in person, on the phone, or over video, a salesperson needs to know when it's right to move from the sales pitch to closing the deal. There's only so much selling you can do. At some point, the customer is going to have to tell you yes or no."
— Grant Cardone

Always remember, the purpose of a text message to set up a phone call and lock down an appointment. The previous 15 steps will be tremendously helpful in achieving this. Follow them earnestly. Take them seriously. Be tenacious. Be relentless. Be unreasonable. If possible, get them in, without negotiating over distance. Get them in. Remember, it is more important to offer information, than it is to give the information. But there are times when you must do what seems wrong; and give them all the information and go for the close from a distance.

There will be a group of people, however, who will not answer and will not come in. You can blame it Carvana. You can blame it on society. You can blame on Millennials. Blame it on whomever you like. Just know it is a real thing, and don't ignore the fact that customers don't care about your sales process. They care about themselves, of course, and some of them just aren't coming in. *The good news is we can sell them too.*

After you have exhausted all the previous steps, turn your video recorder on and give them the best numbers presentation you can.

This can be very powerful and effective. Make no mistake about it, you can close deals through recorded video. I have done it many times, and you can too. If the customer has a need or a want for your product, they just need to have something to say yes to.

Invest in a tripod and start recording videos of you presenting numbers to "Mr. Customer," through the camera. Look at the camera. Call them by name and go for the close. Customers really appreciate this. Imagine getting home from the kids' soccer practice, looking at your phone and having a video from a smiling, determined, friendly salesperson giving you the price, down payment options, term options and monthly payment options that you wanted. Customers can't buy if they don't know all these things. If they won't come in, you can't sell them anything, UNLESS you go for the close over the phone, and video is the most effective way to close from a distance.

Some people love talking to a camera, and some people don't. I know a lot of salespeople who are much better at presenting numbers to a camera than they are presenting numbers to a live customer face to face. They are bolder and prouder of their figures. If you are one of these people, great! Keep recording and sending videos. It will only make you a better closer.

Of course, there are those who are camera shy and feel uncomfortable on video. Hey, that's okay, too. Record it until you get it right, and don't worry about being perfect. Just get the information to them and ask them to buy. Feel the fear and do it anyway. We must send the video, because they may not answer our phone call, but they will watch the video; and if our numbers make sense and they have a desire to buy our product, they will text us back. And if they don't like our numbers, they will let us know. We've got to have this dialogue to close the deal. If it was easy, everyone would do it, and there wouldn't be much value in it.

Take a deep breath, and press record. You have nothing to lose. They aren't coming in anyway, so your video can't hurt. If they don't respond at first, keep sending videos and offers to them until they buy, die, or block your number. You have nothing to lose.

"Someone is getting closed here. Where is my tripod?" — The Wise Salesman

Chapter 17: Beg

I'm not ashamed to call and plead to you, baby,
If pleading keeps you from walking out that door.
Ain't too proud to beg and you know it ...— The Temptations

Begging works. Begging is simply persistently beseeching someone. If it didn't work, you wouldn't see panhandlers. You wouldn't hear the cries for attention and help around the world. Children would hush after the first time they were told "no." Begging appeals to the soul. People want to help people. Not begging is similar to not asking for the sale. It's a mistake not to ask for the sale. It is wrong not to beg.

Think about the GoFundMe requests for money on the Internet. We've all helped someone who's had a fire, a health disaster, or suffered an injury in a traffic wreck. We're glad to give to worthy cause, but we don't typically give without being asked. The same holds true for sales. You have to ask for what you want. Being polite and direct is vital. Just do it. Don't be too proud to beg. I'll do it first, if it makes you feel better.

"Please share this book with someone you know who is in sales. Please find me on Facebook and like my page. Please follow me on Twitter. Please connect with me on LinkedIn. It would mean the world to me. Please do it for me."

I bet your grandmother even taught you to use your manners and say "please." Persistently say please. Will you please come in today? Will you please ask for me? I know you don't want to pay that much, but please do it anyway. Please do it for me. I really need this deal.

"Please, Mr. Customer, Please!" — *The Wise Salesman*

Chapter 18: Apologize

"An apology is the super glue of life. It can repair just about anything." – Lynn Johnston, award-winning cartoonist.

Oftentimes, two-way text messaging goes dormant. The prospect just stops texting you. You have made Big Offers, Big Claims, sent pictures, and videos. You have called numerous times and left Big Claims on their voicemail. But they have gone silent. Nothing.

It is time to apologize. Apologize for what? You haven't done anything wrong! That may be true, but it doesn't matter. If you want them to respond, it is time to apologize. Apologizing stirs up emotions. If you have a stale conversation, simply apologize, as if you did something to cause the conversation to stall. Whether you did or not, does not matter. Apologizing makes you seem a less like a salesperson, and this is important. Everybody likes to buy, but nobody likes to be sold. Be the anti-salesman and apologize. Get the conversation going again. This is a big deal. Don't let pride get in the way of getting them in your showroom. Apologize. Very often when you do, they will call immediately, to see what you are talking about. Anytime a customer is calling it is a good thing. You can make them a Big Offer and go for the appointment.

"I am so sorry, John. Was it something I said? Please forgive me. Please text me back." :(

This works more than 70 percent of the time. They might say, *"Who is this?"* or *"What are you talking about?"* to which I always reply, *"We were having such a good conversation, chatting back and forth about cars and then, POOF! You were gone! Was it something I said? I promise I won't do it again."*

"No, no, I just got busy with the kids," or *"I just haven't had time."* Whatever they say now, they are talking again, and we can make another Big Offer to get them back in our game.

"Whew, I thought you were mad at me." :/ "I am so glad you aren't. Have you heard about the Huge Sales Event we have going on?"

I have an apology video that I sent to 1,000 dealers at one time on my YouTube channel. Search for: *Billy W Merritt. It is OK to say, I Am Sorry.*

I sent out this simple video apology, and I got 22 responses from dealers across the country. That is a very low response rate, right? What if I told you that three of them did business with me, and that total revenue was $126,000 from those three events. All from a 60-second apology that cost me nothing.

"I am more than happy to apologize for something I had no idea I did or didn't do. I am sorry." — The Wise Salesman

Chapter 19: Be Patiently Persistent

"The key to feeding yourself is patience, and that doesn't come naturally. You have to work at it." — Gary Vaynerchuck, Belarusian-American entrepreneur

Some text message customers are low funnel. They are ready to buy, and you can sell them in a short period of time. Those are the fun ones. Others take time, sometimes a long time. This road makes more turns and can be unpredictable. And the long road can be longer than you expect. It takes way more effort than most people think. It takes an average of twelve text messages and four phone calls to get an appointment, and half of the appointments don't show up the first time. It takes patience, with persistent action. Take the long view. We can't close everyone today. That is why our pipeline must stay full, so we can close someone today. Close the ones we can and move all the others one step further down the road to the sale — Destination Delivery. That guy is on the Soooold Train!

I have had text conversations for months, before customers came in and bought. Your pipeline must be full to the point of overflowing, so you can afford to put in the time it takes to nurture, and eventually move, customers. Hang in there. Think in these terms. *"I am going to get this customer in here no matter what it takes, or how long it takes. I am in this for the long haul."*

Some customers will get emotional. Some customers will complain. Some customers will lead you on a wild goose chase or lie to you. Some customers will waste your time. Don't give up on them. Hang in there and win, by closing the distance and then closing the deal. Be forgiving. Remain positive. Stick to the rules and be patient. Giving up early ensures defeat. Hanging in for the long haul gives you a shot. Keep working the lead. If you take enough well-placed shots, you will hit your target and get the appointment.

In 2007, I founded Unlimited Marketing Solutions. I called on new car dealers across the country, pitching them on allowing me to host staffed events and special sales. I made some very big claims. I called on the big dealers — successful ones. I made voice calls. I made video calls. I sent thousands of emails. I send thousands of text messages every day.

There was this one dealer I really wanted to work with. David Karangu is a Kenyan-born immigrant who has made a fortune in the car business. I really admired his story. In 1985, David started washing cars at Florida car dealership. In 2007, David Karangu sold his Mercedes Benz, BMW, Ford, VW, Subaru and other dealerships, and retired at age 40 as a self-made multi-millionaire. He then relocated to Atlanta, Ga. from Augusta, Ga. Before settling in Atlanta, he took a world tour and then built his house — one of the biggest homes in Atlanta.

By mid-2010, he found himself pulled back to the business he fell in love with when he was 18. He started buying new car franchises in the Atlanta area. I was determined to do an event for David Karangu. I called every day. I sent emails every day. With the email technology I use, I could tell he was opening them.

I ultimately got his cell number and I started texting. I followed the rules of this book. Finally, four months after I started reaching out to him, I did the first of several events for Mr. Karangu. You can see one of the videos that I sent him, titled, "Billy W. Merritt Big Event Claims," You can also find a video titled, "I am Obsessed With You," that I filmed at David's dealership, while we were hosting one of the big events.

It took a lot of patience to acquire Mr. Karangu as a customer, but it was worth it. Sometimes, patience is indeed a virtue. That is, patience with persistent action.

"I have been doing this a long time and I am going to keep doing what I know is the right thing to do. Persist with action and patience." — *The Wise Salesman*

Chapter 20. Ask for Referrals and Testimonials

"People influence people. Nothing influences people more than a recommendation from a trusted friend. A trusted referral influences people more than the best broadcast message. A trusted referral is the Holy Grail of advertising." — Mark Zuckerberg, CEO, Facebook

"92% of respondents reported that a positive recommendation from a friend, family member, or someone they trust, is the biggest influence on whether they buy a product or service."

Highly Recommended: *Harnessing the Power of Word of Mouth and Social Media to Build Your Brand and Your Business— Paul M. Rand,*

A beautiful business model is a business that creates customers, who create customers. In the business of referrals, trust is the most important reason a recommendation is made, and, conversely, lack of trust the single greatest reason referrals don't happen. Be trustworthy. Give them a reason to give you a referral. Word of mouth is the best form of advertising. A customer talking about their experience with you is worth ten times that which you say about yourself. We need to take such great care of our customers that they tell the whole world about us. Make sure everyone gets the VIP Treatment. Make sure you treat everyone like millionaires. Except for millionaires; we treat them like billionaires. Be remarkable. Be remembered. Be referred.

Consider giving referral fees. Consider giving really big referral fees. Every problem can be fixed with the right incentive. Cash in hand seems to be a pretty good incentive to most people. Don't just offer referral fees to those who bought from you. Make a big deal about paying referral fees to anyone who sends someone your way. We need everyone to know about you. Who should we ask for referrals? Everyone.

Most agree that a happy customer will recommend you if asked, but an unsatisfied customer is going to tell everyone. This makes it very important to get as many people as possible speaking positively on your behalf, and they aren't going to do it unless you ask them to.

A very powerful and fun way to do this, is to offer a discount for a video endorsement. Having a trouble closing the deal? Give an additional $500 "Facebook personal endorsement video discount." Record them explaining why they did business with you, and why someone else should do business with you. Put this video on YouTube, Facebook, and your website. Have them put it on their personal social media pages. The bigger collection of customer videos you have, the more powerful your marketing will be. You can get a third-party endorsement and referral any time, by simply sharing the video again.

As soon as you ink the deal, ask for a five-star review from the customer. Have them do it in front of you, before they leave. Have them do it on Facebook and Google. Make sure that potential customers see that others are happy to endorse you.

There are reputation management companies that people and other businesses pay to manage their ratings and reviews. This is so unnecessary. Manage your own reviews, ratings and reputation. Give a VIP treatment to everyone and make sure you get the five-star review. Get the testimonial. Ask for a testimonial video and five-star Google and Facebook review every single time. You need to have so many awesome reviews that even if you somehow got a less than a five-star review, it wouldn't negatively affect your overall score. The only way to do this is the make referrals a top priority. Ask for them every time.

In fact, we can even use Mass Text and ask everyone at one time.

"Hey, this is Billy. I am reaching out to see if you know anyone who would be interested in our latest offer. We are currently selling all our cars at wholesale prices. Plus, for a limited time, we are paying an extra $4,000 for every trade-in. This is a really big deal.

Do you know anyone who would want to take advantage of this, before it is too late?
Your net worth is your network. Use your text lists to ask for referrals .

"There are 8 billion people on the planet, and I am going to ask all 8 billion for a referral." -The Wise Salesman

Chapter 21: Make Mistakes

"Anyone who has never made a mistake has never tried anything new." — Albert Einstein

"Even a mistake may turn out to be the one thing necessary to a worthwhile achievement." --Henry Ford

There are only two ways you can fail at this.

1. Don't try.

2. Quit.

Your best teacher is very often your last mistake. These rules work, but you won't fully understand until you put them in action. You have to use them consistently. You have to start and be patiently persistent. You don't, however, have to be perfect.

I once hired two salespeople, Roger and Caesar. Both young, and both eager. They went through the same training process, which revolves heavily around text message and phone skills.

Honestly, Roger had way more skills, ability and potential. He was naturally easy to talk to, and charming. He was amazing with his customers, handling customer complaints and objections with ease and confidence. He spoke to everyone with a calm smile and could close anyone.

Caesar had a thick accent and was naturally shy. It was obvious that he was nervous when confronted with customer complaints and problems. Caesar would most likely never be a powerful closer.

During the time I led both these young men, Caesar sold twice as many cars as Roger. How could this be?

Here's how: I never could get Roger to make enough calls, though there was no one I would rather have speak to my customers. I contribute it to laziness or lack of hunger, or both. Whether that is accurate or not, Caesar paid zero attention to Roger, and put 100 percent of his attention and energy into texting and calling customers. He made mistakes. He made lots of mistakes, but he never quit texting, calling, making big claims and following up. When he ran into a problem, he would say in his thick accent, *"Billy, can you help me with this one?"*

"Sure," I said every time, because I was so excited that though he was fearful, he made the calls anyway. Sometimes, I would jump in and text or call the customer myself. We sold a lot of cars.

"Good job, Caesar!" I would say, *"Now go make some more mistakes."*

Caesar wasn't afraid to make mistakes, and you shouldn't be either. Grab your phone and make some calls. Send some texts and make some mistakes. Your manager, your family, and your customers will appreciate it.

"I am pretty sure I know what I am doing here. If not, I am going to do it anyway." —The Wise Salesman

Chapter 22. Text Them One More Time

"Our greatest weakness lies in giving up. The most certain way to succeed is always to try just one more time." -- Thomas A. Edison

"Just Do It." --Nike

You can't go wrong following the advice of one of the most important inventors in history, or one of the most successful businesses in history. Just do it, and then do it again, and again. Always do it one more time. Remember, sometimes the long road is longer than you expected. You must endure to persevere. Don't stop. Don't quit. Keep chopping wood. Finish the drill. Do good work. Follow the rules. Stay positive. Stay focused. Be bold. Be confident. Repeat. Just make another text. You have nothing to lose, and everything to gain. It doesn't cost a thing and there is no reason not to do it. Just make another text. Just one more. After that, do it one more time. After that, once more. After that... Yep! Again.

"I am going to text this guy again." The Wise Salesman

Chapter 23. Make One More Call

I can accept failure, but I can't accept not trying. -- Michael Jordan

I've always believed that if you put in the work, the results will come. -- The World's Greatest

Some people want it to happen, some wish it would happen, others make it happen. -- #23

I've failed -over, and over, and over again, in my life and that is why I succeed. -- M.J.

Obstacles don't have to stop you. If you run into a wall, don't turn around and give up. Figure out how to climb it, go through it, or work around it. -- The GOAT

You have to expect things of yourself before you can do them. --Air Jordan

23 is my favorite number. It was Michael Jordan's number. Every quote above was made by Michael Jordan. He will always be the greatest in my mind. He was my favorite basketball player, so I dedicated my favorite chapter to my favorite basketball player - 23 to 23. We have saved the best for last.

It may seem funny that I am obsessed with calling customers, yet I wrote a book about texting them. But remember: the purpose of a text message is to set up a phone call to set an appointment. I can't stress enough how important it is to call your customers. And trust me, I stress it every day. I am stressing it to you again, right now. Make another call. Call them one more time. Be like Mike. Don't accept not trying one more time. Make another call. Be like Mike, put in the work. Be like Mike. Put in the work. Make another call. BE like Mike. Fail enough to succeed. Make another call.

This is so important that you must make it a huge priority. You can't shoot from the hip by making a call or two here, and a call or two there. You must make it a big part of your day, and a huge part of your success plan. Don't take the phone call lightly. Call them all, and then call them all one more time. Sit down. Block out an hour of time for nothing but calls, and make one more call over and over, for an hour.

Your boss needs you to do it. Your company needs you to do it. Your family needs you to do it, your church needs you to do it. Your community needs you to do it. The economy needs you to do it. The world needs you to do it. The entire economy of the world is built upon sales and is built upon calling customers. You need to do this for yourself, too. Make one more call.

"I am going to call the guy one more time." The Wise Salesman entire economy of the world is built upon sales and is built upon calling customers. You need to do this for yourself, too. Make one more call.

"I am going to call the guy one more time." The Wise Salesman

Conclusion

Texting is Serious Business

Texting is a serious and lucrative business, and those who master The Art of Text Message Selling will reap the rewards. I want you to decide right now that you are going to make texting a priority. You must take it seriously, and act. The knowledge is not enough. You must engage in consistent, massive action.

I already know a great deal about you. You seriously want to be great at sales, or else you wouldn't have picked up this book, and you definitely wouldn't have read it all the way to the conclusion. You are here to do great things and make your mark on your industry. We have a lot in common. You are a serious businessperson. I am honored to call you a kindred spirit. When you start taking your business seriously, you will be criticized and hated on. That is the path to success. Ignore the nonsense and carry on. Take it seriously, but don't take yourself too seriously. Keep it light and have fun. Memorize the Rules and when you are having trouble, ask yourself if you have tried them all.

1. Make a Big Offer.
2. Be Fast.
3. Have a Great Attitude.
4. Send Photos, Video and Make Another Big Offer.
5. Stop Texting and Start Calling.
6. Leave a Voicemail.
7. Keep Sending Information, and Lots of it.
8. Sell the Appointment and Lock It Down.
9. Get Social
10. Use Positive Language.
11. Carefully Copy and Paste.
12. Love the One You are With.

13. Overcome Objections.
14. Use Mass Text.
15. Send Them a Secure Online Credit App.
16. Go for the Video Close.
17. Beg.
18. Apologize.
19. Be Patiently Persistent.
20. Ask for Referrals and testimonials.
21. Make Mistakes.
22. Text Them One More Time.
23. Make One More Call.

From one fanatical sales person to another, I wish you the best, and hope to hear from you soon. Enjoy, use, and share this information with all who are interested in The Art of Text Message Selling.

Sincerely, Billy W. Merritt

Acknowledgements

When I sat down to make note of everyone for whom I am grateful for this accomplishment, I became overwhelmed. Acknowledging everyone who helped me gain this knowledge, and then put this specialized knowledge in order was a difficult task. So many people have played so many roles. I will not be able to mention each and every person than helped and inspired me. The task is too daunting. Just know that for each of you, I am so grateful. You are all rock stars in "My Book.": I have to start at home, to acknowledge those who mean the most to me.

First, my family. Of course, this begins with the love of my life, my beautiful wife, April Ann, who I love for her brilliance and her beauty. She inspires me. She keeps me grounded. She is a real-life dream partner. She's my girl. Thank you to her parents, Bobby and Janice for creating and raising such an amazing woman. You are two amazing, loving, kind, gentle, souls.

To each of our four children, Cooper, you are brilliant and hard-working with dreams and ambitions. That is every parent's dream for their children. Case, I love your imagination and you have the heart of a champion. Our little talks are priceless to me. Trevor, your determination is something I marvel at. That, with your talent will take you wherever you want to go. Chloe, you are pure love. I am so glad you found me. You all give me a reason to be more. And to the lady who loved me first, my mom, Dawn, who sacrificed so much to give me a decent chance at life. Your love made it all possible. To my dad, Bill, who taught me so much and wanted more for me than he ever had, thank you. To my other dad, Danny, for loving my mom and taking care of us. To my great grandmother, Marie, the strongest person I ever met. To my grandmother, Wilholmina, for planting your heart of gold in all of us. To all my brothers and sisters, Dori, Dustin, Meagan, Amy, Kathi, Tyler, and

Joshua. Thank you for sharing your parents with me. I am grateful for you all.

To my core team, Joey and Hank. You made this possible and proved its value by putting the Art of Text Message Selling into action. Thank you for believing in me. I believe in you. Thank you to Ron Davis for hiring me into the car business in 1996 and encouraging me to this day. You are a true friend and brother. To Michael Carson, who believed in me and gave me the first chance to prove my product's value in the marketplace. To Ken Helm, who took me out the dealership and into the dealer services business. I learned a lot from you, Kenny. To my editors, Peter Salinas and Kathleen Rothenberger. To all my teachers in the public education system of Georgia. There are too many people to mention, and I surely left out many who have helped me get here. Thanks to you all. It is my sincere privilege to give you this work.

Thanks,

 Billy W. Merritt
(912)381-9078

About the Author

Billy W. Merritt was born in the small town of Douglas, Ga, on Sept. 20, 1974. His father, a salesman for roofing and construction jobs, had a key impact on his life and future career as an automobile retailer. Billy's father sold the construction jobs by going door-to-door and took Billy along with him. Later, his stepfather, who sold horses along the East Coast, also took him on sales calls.

Sales quickly became part of Billy's DNA, and he became obsessed with the intricacies of sales, and with his innate gift of communicating effectively to close a deal. He also loved cars, which his parents recognized and helped him to amass a huge collection of Hot Wheels cars, and he also bought and meticulously assembled hundreds of model kit cars.

At just 16 years old, Billy began selling roofing and construction jobs, as well as trading horses and coonhounds. His entrepreneurial spirit grew, and at 21 years old he had a thriving hand car wash and detail shop that serviced all the local car dealers in Douglas. This exposed him to car sales on both the front and back end of the business, and he spend many hours in showrooms, detail shops, and service bays. The retail automotive business excited him, so he sold his successful detail business and took a position selling cars. It a great decision. He quickly ascended through the ranks of finance manager, used car manager, new car manager, sales manager, eventually general manager, and later, an owner.

He discovered over his 22-year automotive career was that his main expertise was in marketing, coaching, and sales training. He spent more than five years studying under the greats in the business and attending seminars, taking a variety of courses, and studied at several online sales universities. He worked diligently to find the best-of-the-best practices and tools.

As social media grew to prominence in all aspects of consumer behavior, Billy carefully examined the new marketplace and its potential for automotive marketing. With the rise of social media combined with the impact of millennial buyers on sales in general, Billy instinctively knew he should heavily invest in research on digital advertising and text message marketing.

He amassed a vast knowledge of specialized information that has dramatically changed the way hundreds of dealerships across the country market their businesses and reach consumers. This new paradigm has not only changed how dealers market their business, it's changed the way consumers research and buy their vehicles. This knowledge has been precisely articulated here in this book, and those who take the time to read, understand, and put this powerful information into practice will attract more customers, close more often, and both they and their clients will be more satisfied with the results.

Made in the USA
San Bernardino, CA
28 February 2020